THE BIG BIG BIG CHRISTMAS

written by Mei Shan Dibble

Illustrated by Emma Randall

This is our gingerbread house.

It is big. Really big.

It is so big that we could have it for breakfast, lunch, and dinner.

Our gingerbread house is big.

But not as big as...

Our cat, Freddie!

He is so big that he can't fit through his cat flap and has to tap on the window to be let in.

Freddie is big.

But not as big as...

My guitar teacher, Mr Spinelli!

He is so big that when he gets excited he knocks all the decorations off the mantlepiece.

Mr Spinelli is big.

But not as big as...

It is so big that she hides behind it every morning to jump out and scare the postman.

Mrs McGeachie's snowman is big.

But not as big as...

The Christmas tree in our town square!

It is so big that Mr de Silva had to use his really, really, really tall ladder to put the star on top.

The town Christmas tree is big.

But not as big as...

The Statue of Liberty is so big that if you wanted to knit it a Christmas jumper, you'd need 52 grannies to help.

The Statue of Liberty is big.

But not as big as...

… Mount Everest!

Mount Everest is so big that

if you climbed to the top you could play

rock,
paper,
scissors
with people flying in planes.

Mount Everest is big.

But not as big as…

The ocean!

The ocean is so big that there's enough water in it to have a world-wide water fight.

The ocean is big.

But not as big as...

The sun!

The sun is so big that you could use it to toast ten million marshmallows all in one go.

The sun is big.

But even though God is so big,

he made himself smaller

than our gingerbread house.

He became a tiny baby called Jesus, wrapped up all cosy in cloth and placed in a manger.

This was the very first Christmas.

And why did the bigger-than-even-the-universe God become a tiny baby? Because he had a big job to do. It was so big only he could do it.

He came to rescue people like us

so we could know him now and for always.

That's better than big, shiny presents and lovelier than the cosiest Christmas.

An angel appeared to Joseph and told him that Mary "will give birth to a son. You will name the son Jesus. Give him that name because he will save his people from their sins."

MATTHEW 1:21